Step-*by*-Step
CARDMAKING

GLENNIS GILRUTH

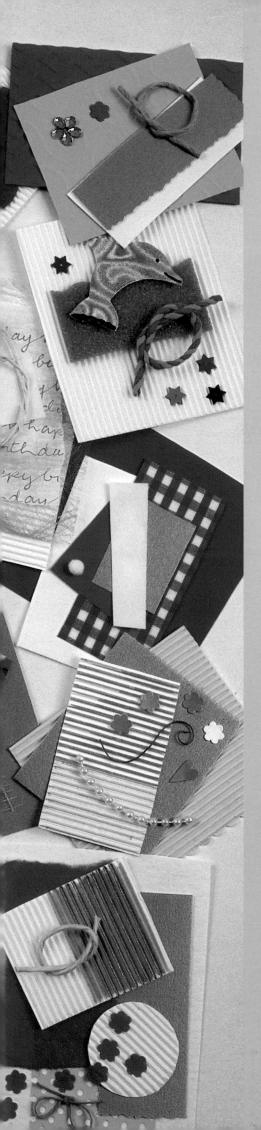

Step-_by_-Step
CARDMAKING

GLENNIS GILRUTH

GUILD OF MASTER CRAFTSMAN PUBLICATIONS

First published 2004 by

Guild of Master Craftsman Publications Ltd

166 High Street, Lewes

East Sussex, BN7 1XU

ISBN 1 86108 440 4

British Cataloguing in Publication Data

A catalogue record of this book is available from the British Library.

Publisher: Paul Richardson

Art Director: Ian Smith

Managing Editor: Gerrie Purcell

Production Manager: Hilary MacCallum

Photographer: Anthony Bailey

Editor: Clare Miller

Art Editor: Gilda Pacitti

Colour reproduction by Icon Reproduction

Printed and bound by Stamford Press

Although care has been taken to ensure that the imperial measurements are true and accurate, they are only conversions from metric; they have been rounded up or down to the nearest $1/8$in, or to the nearest convenient equivalent in cases where the metric measurements themselves are only approximate. When following the projects, use either the metric or the imperial measurements; do not mix units.

CONTENTS

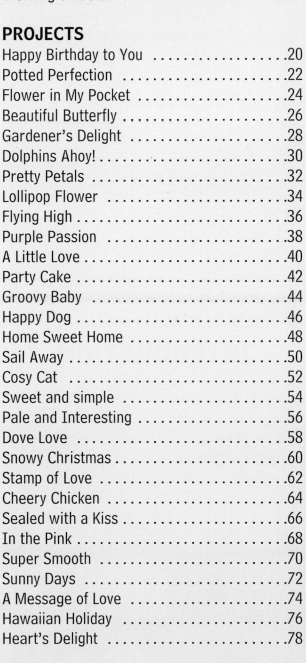

ABOUT THE AUTHOR

Glennis Gilruth is a successful designer and writer, whose obvious love of her work translates in her fresh, fun and easy-to-do designs.

Having gained her degree in Surface Pattern, which incorporates textile design, decorative illustration and 3D design, Glennis began working in the greeting card industry. She is now an established contributor to leading craft magazines, creating papercaft, needlework and mixed media projects. This is her third book.

INTRODUCTION

If you have always wanted to create handmade greeting cards, but didn't know where to begin, I hope you will let me show you just how easy and enjoyable cardmaking can be. Each project has a list of equipment and materials that you will need, plus step-by-step photographs and instructions to guide you on your way to success.

Using easy techniques, beautiful materials and simple shapes, you will soon be making your very own stylish cards for all those special occasions when you want to convey your good wishes, greetings and sentiments to family and friends.

And for those of you who are already happily established in this creative and productive craft, I hope this book of designs will give you plenty of fresh ideas to develop this most pleasurable of pastimes.

Equipment

When you decide that cardmaking is the pastime for you (and I'm sure that you will!) a good starting point is to put together a basic tool kit. Even if you are new to cardmaking you will probably find that you already have many of the following items around your home.

BASIC TOOL KIT

1 Small, sharp scissors for detailed shapes.

2 Larger scissors for straight cuts on larger pieces of paper and card.

3 Plastic ruler and propelling pencil for measuring and ruling lines. A plastic ruler is easy to read and easy to keep clean, and the fine point of a propelling pencil will help you to mark measurements with precision.

4 Clean, soft eraser that will be kind to delicate papers.

5 Assortment of crayons, felt brush pens and gel pens. These are easily available in many different styles from plain to sparkly to pearly; try to find as many as you can.

Most of the items for your basic tool kit can probably be found around your home

6 Paper piercer or a darning needle.

7 Use the above with an old mousemat for making small holes in paper. Use it upside down and the foam layer will allow the needle to slide easily through the paper, whilst the plastic layer will protect your work surface.

8 Empty ball-point pen to use as a stylus to impress lines before making folds.

9 Spoon to smooth along folds and give a clean and crisp finish.

10 Adhesives – I've used three types of adhesive: double-sided adhesive tape, PVA craft adhesive and sticky foam pads. Each has a particular use and, in the instructions for each design, I will suggest which one to use. Read more about these adhesives in the 'Techniques' section.

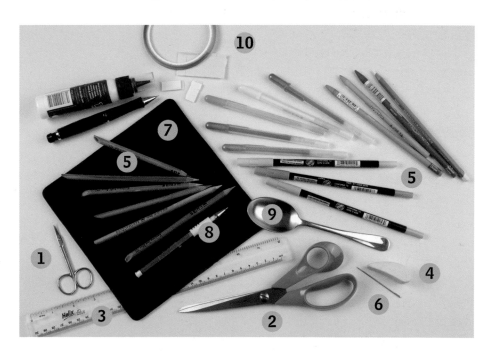

EXTRA EQUIPMENT

Whilst your basic tool kit will always be indispensable to you, and many of the cards in this book can be created with just scissors and adhesive, the following extra pieces of equipment will enable you to make each and every design in this book.

1 Craft knife – useful when making slick, straight cuts or trimming the edges of cards.

2 Metal safety ruler with finger protection – essential when cutting straight edges with a craft knife.

3 Cutting mat – will protect your work surface and keep the knife blade sharp.

4 Rotary cutter – ideal for making precise, straight cuts in card and paper. It can replace the craft knife, metal ruler and cutting mat, and is no danger to worktops or fingers!

5 Craft punches – similar to ordinary hole punches, these are used to cut paper into decorative shapes and borders.

6 Decorative scissors – available in many patterns from deckle to zig zag and ideal for trimming panels and edges.

7 Round-nose pliers – invaluable if you want to work with craft wire. They'll help you to cut wire neatly and accurately, and make perfect curls and scrolls.

8 Light box – a great help when tracing shapes and templates, and it's essential if you'd like to try embossing, using brass stencils.

9 Ball-end stylus – for use with the light box and brass stencils.

10 Crimper – to make decorative, grooved paper.

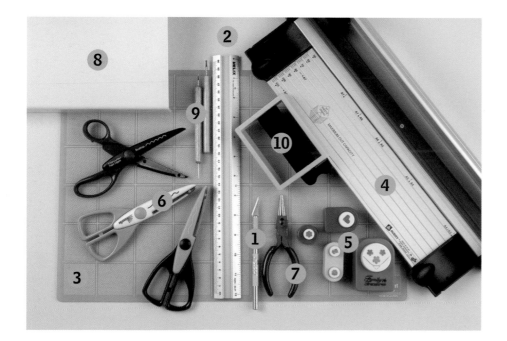

This extra equipment allows boundless possibilities in cardmarking

SAFETY NOTES

Knives and scissors

Sharp knives and scissors are easier to use than blunt ones but accidents can happen so, when cutting, bear the following rules in mind:

- find a firm and tidy work surface

- never cut directly towards yourself

- never cut against a plastic ruler with a craft knife because the blade can easily cut into the ruler and there is no protection for your fingers

- if cutting against a ruler, always use a metal safety ruler that protects your fingers

- never use a piece of wood as a cutting mat because the wood will grip the blade and make it difficult to control

- when not in use, retract knife blades or replace blade covers

- keep all sharp implements, such as scissors, needles and knives away from the edge of your work surface, preferably in a tray or box

- dispose of used blades carefully.

Adhesives and colouring materials

Make sure you have read and understood the manufacturer's recommendations regarding use and storage before you start working with adhesives and paints.

General

When creating your cards, ensure that all parts of the design are firmly attached, especially beads, wire or small metal parts. Apart from the disappointment of your design falling apart, there is a danger that children and pets will swallow pieces. Never give cards with attached pieces of decoration or beads to very small children.

When using the ball-end of a stylus, it is a good idea to cork the sharp point that is facing towards you.

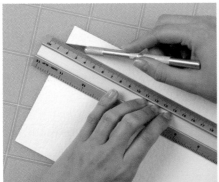
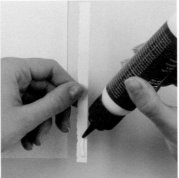

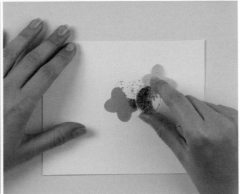

Cardmaking Materials

Retailers are offering ever-expanding ranges of art and craft materials

Cardmaking is such a popular pastime that manufacturers and retailers are responding with ever-expanding ranges of fabulous art and craft materials, and always with an eye to current fashion, so it's easy to keep your cards looking up-to-the-minute. I have used materials which are readily available in shops and by mail order but if you encounter difficulty in obtaining identical materials, please don't be discouraged; each and every component can easily be replaced by something similar and you'll still get beautiful, professional results. I've used some of the materials on more than one design to show you how versatile they can be. The main thing is to be creative and have fun!

An A4 sheet of paper or metre of ribbon will go a long way when cardmaking so you will soon build up quite a collection and whilst it's hugely enjoyable to shop for brand new packs of card, gleaming pearly paper and packets of beads and sequins, it's also fun to forage for likely looking materials at home. Lovely scraps of card and paper can be salvaged from food packaging, confectionery and toiletries, whilst beads and jewels can be rescued from old clothes.

You can save money on materials for cardmaking by recycling packaging and parts from old clothes and costume jewellery

Plain gift wrap is a useful source of coloured paper and it's quite inexpensive, so you can snip away without breaking the bank. If you are looking for ribbons, cords, or pretty motifs, keep an eye on bargain bins in shops and markets where you can find inexpensive jewellery and hair decorations which you can take apart and re-use as decorations on your cards. You can also save money and build up a super stash of materials by finding cardmaking friends who will share packs of paper and card, or swap goodies with you.

Paper and card
Available in abundance in shops and by mail order. There are many other sheet materials such as foam, weaves, mesh, netting, even lightweight wood veneer.

Strings 'n' things
These are available by the metre or yard, and there are so many of them that it's difficult to know where to begin! From threads, to paper cord, to braids, there are hundreds from which to choose. Ribbon is a great way to introduce fabric to your designs and if you bond it to paper, using double-sided adhesive tape, you can cut shapes without fraying.

Beads, jewels and sequins

Although cheap and plentiful these will add priceless sparkle to your greeting cards and can be sewn, threaded, tied or glued onto your designs.

Glitter

This is another accessory which can add the sparkle factor. Look around for fine-format glitters in designer colours. As an alternative to glitter, you can use miniscule no-hole glass beads, such as Accent beads, which are available in a wide range of colours. Both glitter and Accent beads adhere very well to double-sided adhesive tape and PVA adhesive.

Die-cuts

These are machine-cut shapes of any sheet material such as paper, card, foam or even wood. They make a very useful addition to the cardmaker's kit and if you take care to incorporate them fully into your designs, by use of colour or decoration, they'll look as if they really belong.

Craft wire

The smooth and metallic version forms lovely scrolls and curls, while the rustic paper-covered version is ideal for flower stems. There are also spiral-effect wires which can be unravelled and wound around shapes or teased into motifs.

A tiny sequin is wonderful for adding that little extra detail

You can also create your own die-cuts using paper punches

Making Wire Curls and Scrolls

To make the curls and scrolls for the projects in this book, all you will need is a pair of round-nose pliers.

1 Make the curls at either end of the wire first.
2 Then make a smooth bend in the length of the wire.
3 Twist the wire in the middle so that the curls face in opposite directions and you have made a perfect scroll.

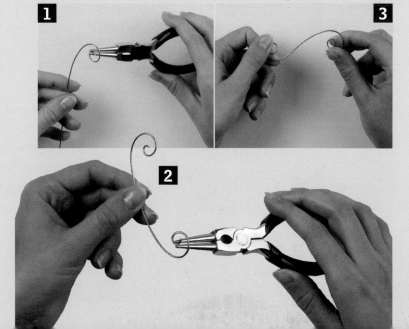

10 IDEAS FOR CHOOSING AND USING YOUR MATERIALS

1 You'd be amazed at how many designs you can rustle up from offcuts and scraps, so don't throw them away.

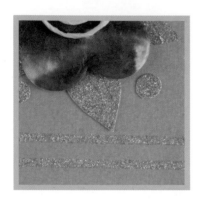

2 As you gather together your cardmaking equipment and materials, do take time to play with them and get to know them. Spread out paper and card, tie knots in threads, scribble with crayons and run your fingers through those beads. This isn't wasting your materials, it's getting to know them!

3 Use narrow double-sided adhesive tape to make super-fine glittery stripes, or cover scraps of coloured card with double-sided tape, sprinkle with glitter, and cut out sparkling motifs.

4 Try cutting paper and card with decorative scissors, and try tearing and folding it. Do some tear more easily than others?

5 Lay papers, ribbons and fabrics together and see how they interact, visually. Which colours and textures do you like?

6 Make a few curls of wire and thread a few beads. Have you got the bead bug yet?

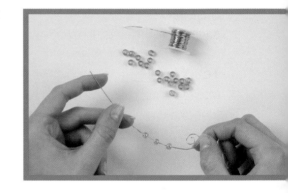

7 Leaves can be cut from ribbon bonded to paper.

8 Try doodling with various pens and notice how different cards and papers react. Is the ink easily absorbed by the paper or is it taking a long time to dry?

9 Small fabric flowers are great for cardmaking but the plastic centres can spoil the look so remove them and glue the petal layers together in the centre, then add a small blob of PVA and sprinkle with Accent beads.

10 It's fun to handle all these different craft materials and whilst you are experimenting with them and moving them around you may spot interesting colour combinations or intriguing partnerships of paper and other materials. At this point you could make little visual reminders by taking a few snippets and sticking these onto pieces of card, for later reference. In this way, you will build up a resource of ideas, much as an artist keeps a sketchbook.

Techniques

CUTTING, TEARING AND FOLDING

Straight cutting

Whilst most of the cuts on your card designs can be freehand, you will need to make more precise, straight cuts when making card blanks, using scissors, a knife or a rotary cutter.

Detailed cutting

All of the more detailed shapes in the projects in this book were cut with a pair of small, sharp scissors. I find that small, curved embroidery scissors are unbeatable when cutting intricate shapes.

For a smooth finish, always work in one direction and move the paper around, rather than moving around the paper.

Tearing

Most paper today is machine made, which results in the minute fibres of the paper laying in one direction, giving it a grain. This makes it easier to tear with the grain but when working on a small scale, as in cardmaking, this is not a problem.

When tearing a small panel, rather than trying to follow a ruled line, use a similar-sized piece of paper as a guide.

Folding

As with tearing, paper also folds more easily in the direction of the grain but, again, for small-scale work such as cardmaking, this is not a problem.

For the perfect fold, take a stylus or empty ball-point pen and, with the aid of a ruler, run it along the fold line. I find that it doesn't really matter which side of the card you rule with the stylus, but if folding glazed, pearl or metallic card I always rule on the reverse because it can damage the surface colour on those finishes.

Carefully make the fold, pressing, rather than rubbing it and then place a clean sheet of paper over the fold and smooth it down with the back of a spoon (top left and right, page 14).

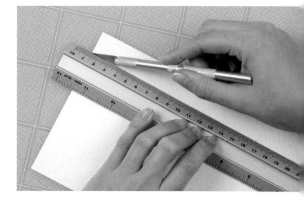

When using a craft knife, always use a metal safety ruler to protect your fingers and a plastic cutting mat to protect your table

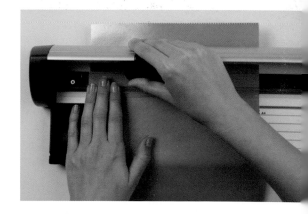

For straight cuts, a great alternative to both scissor and knife is the rotary cutter. It'll be kind to fingers and worktops, and if you are lucky enough to have one of these you will be able to make straight, right-angled cuts with ease

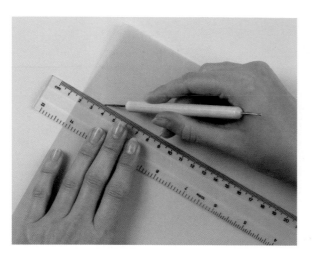

Make folds in card using a ruler and a stylus

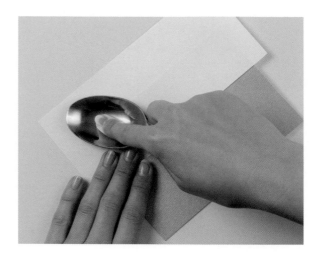

Smooth the fold with the back of a spoon

Try drawing felt pens and gel pens along the grooves of corrugated card to create fascinating stripes

ADDING COLOUR

In addition to buying coloured paper and card for use in your designs, you can colour scraps of paper and card yourself using different types of pen. Try felt brush pens, which handle almost like watercolour paints, and gel pens which are available in many different styles from plain, to pearly, to sparkly. These coloured scraps will make beautiful background panels or can be cut into flowers and other motifs.

STAMPING, EMBOSSING AND STENCILLING

Stamping, embossing and stencilling could be seen as specialist separate crafts but now that there are so many stamps, ink pads and stencils around for you to choose from you can mix and match elements of these techniques into your designs. I find that it's much easier to create these effects on separate panels or scraps which I can then incorporate into a card design, rather than work straight onto the card.

Rubber stamping

Stamping can be applied to almost any flat card, paper or material, though glossy surfaces may require a special ink pad. It's important to keep the stamp clean to ensure a crisp image, so keep the colour in the ink pads fresh by cleaning the stamp each time you change colour. Successful stamping requires even inking of the stamp, even pressure (not too heavy or you will distort the image) and, finally, clean removal of the stamp, without smudging. With a little practice you can get a good result almost every time. If stamping grabs you, you might want to try embossing ink pads and powders which, when warmed with a specialist craft heating tool, can be used to give a raised shiny or sparkly effect.

You can make pretty background papers with just a small stamp

Embossing

Embossed or raised areas feature on many commercially produced cards and add an extra dimension to a design. You can emboss card and paper by hand using brass stencils which are thin panels of brass with finely cut motifs. You will also need a small light box and a ball-end stylus.

Secure the stencil to the right side of the card using a small piece of adhesive tape. Place it on the light box, stencil side down, and light will shine through the cut-away areas of the stencil and through the card so that you can see the design quite clearly. Run a ball-end stylus around the edges of the cut away areas and the design will begin to form on the right side of the paper.

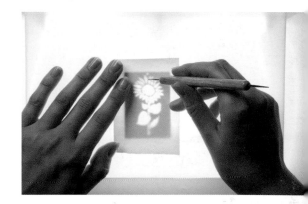

Use a light box and the ball-end of a stylus to create an embossed image

Stencilling

Even the simplest stencilled design has appeal and, as with stamping, there are many designs and colouring materials to choose from. When stencilling, the main thing to remember is that the best results are achieved with a gradual approach. You can always add more colour but you can't take it away if a heavy application of colour leaks under the stencil.

I kept the brass stencil in position after embossing this flower and used mini-sponge applicators and ink pads to add colour

15

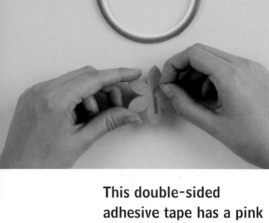

The main aim when glueing is to make a firm, invisible bond whilst using the least possible amount of glue. When cardmaking, this can be achieved by choosing the right glue for the right job and each project in this book contains suggestions about which glue to use for each particular task. I recommend the following glues:

Double-sided adhesive tape is invaluable when assembling cards. It works well on just about every surface, from absorbent to glossy, even wood or plastic.
Plus point It makes an instant bond and there's no drying time.
Minus point Once it takes hold, it's difficult to adjust or remove.

This double-sided adhesive tape has a pink removable backing which is easy to see when the tape is in place

PVA adhesive is a white liquid which dries clear and forms a very strong bond. It can be used on lots of different materials and is ideal when attaching tiny elements of design such as sequins or small punched shapes.
Plus point It's economical, easy to use, and not at all 'stringy'.
Minus point It is a 'wet' glue and can distort paper and card, especially if applied over large areas. It takes a while to dry completely, especially on non-absorbent surfaces such as plastic.

For ease of use, squeeze a little adhesive onto a piece of scrap card and replace the bottle cap immediately. A cocktail stick is great for precision placing of this glue

Sticky foam pads are useful when creating a 3D effect. They form a strong bond and, as double-sided tape, will adhere to just about any material.
Plus point They make an instant bond and there's no drying time.
Minus point Once they take hold, they're difficult to adjust or remove if you find you have placed them incorrectly.

Cut foam pads into strips for small motifs

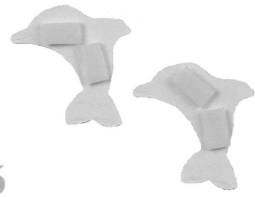

Working on Detail

MOTIFS

Each of the designs in this book has a focal point, a central motif, around which the card is styled. A motif could be anything from a sailing boat to a heart and you can very easily create your own motifs in any craft materials you choose.

Flowers are the most popular motifs to feature on greeting cards and you can make them in minutes.

Animals make people smile and are always in demand on greeting cards but they can be tricky to draw, so keep them simple. Once you've got a shape you like you can scale it up or down. Happy Dog and Cosy Cat, who were inspired by real, live animals, are favourites of mine.

Hearts are wonderful shapes for cardmakers and you can make them in any material and in any colour.

Trains, planes and automobiles, or indeed any kind of vehicle or craft makes a fun motif. I love boats and high-flying kites. These motifs are great for birthdays or wishing someone well as they set out on a journey or in a new career.

ADDING YOUR GREETING

Adding a handwritten greeting is the part that many cardmakers find a bit scary! Let me dispel the myth that only those skilled in calligraphy can add handwriting to their cards. My feeling is that each and every cardmaker's own hand adds charm and originality which is much appreciated by the person who receives the card.

It's easy to style your own handwriting so that it looks good on greeting cards. The first step is to try an assortment of pens. Loosen up and do lots of doodling and writing to get to know which ones suit your hand, and with a bit of practice you will soon be writing key phrases such as 'with love' or 'happy birthday' with ease. The tiny writing I have used on several of my card designs came about through just such a 'doodling' session, when I found that it was much easier to write my greetings on a tiny scale than to make elaborately written captions across my cards. I first tried a finely tipped

Just thread a die-cut flower shape onto a stalk of knotted paper cord and you have a dainty bloom

Add a sense of movement by using curls of wire or tassels

So many pens from which to choose!

17

Peel-off greetings are available for all occasions and in many styles

mapping pen then progressed to an ultra-fine drafting pen which, having an ink cartridge, makes it even easier so, if you get the opportunity, do have a doodle with a fine-nibbed pen. I also like to add writing and small details with gel pens because they are available in such a wide range of colours and styles, such as sparkly or glossy, which can be co-ordinated with the card design.

Many of the cards in this book don't carry a written greeting, but greetings can certainly be added. If you've tried handwriting and don't feel happy with that method you can create text on a home computer, use peel-off lettering or a rubber stamp. Computer-generated text has the advantage of producing any wording you want in thousands of different fonts and colours, and in any size. Each of these methods can be applied directly onto the card blank, or in the form of a decorative panel.

CARD BLANKS AND ENVELOPES

Think about the size and shape of the card and envelope before you start to make the card. If you are sending a lot of cards, say invitations or Christmas cards, ready-made card blanks and envelopes could be quite a time saver. These are available in many different colours and sizes and the designs featured in this book can easily be tailored to fit stock sizes.

Making a Card Blank

A card blank is simply a fold of card and it's very easy and economical to make your own, as follows:

1 Measure and mark two dots for placing the ruler.

2 Using a stylus, or empty ball-point pen, rule a line for the fold.

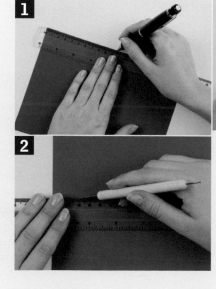

3 Fold the card and smooth the crease with the back of a spoon. Trim the edges if necessary.

Making a Folded Wrapper

For special occasions, why not present your card in a decorative folded wrapper or sleeve? These are easy to make, lots of fun, and will really add the 'wow!' factor to your handmade cards. You can use anything in sheet form from paper, to plastic, to mesh, but do try to co-ordinate with the greeting card, in terms of material, colour and style.

2 Place the card in the centre and wrap it lengthways.

3 Fold ends over and glue or tape them in position, then let the decoration commence!

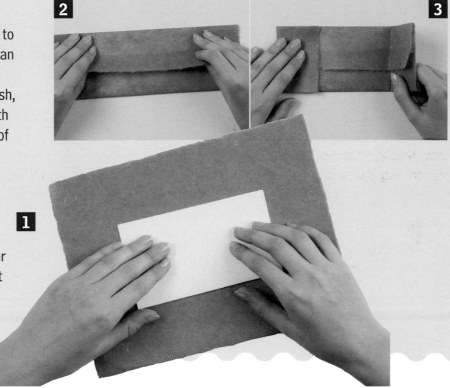

1 Choose a piece of paper or sheet material about twice the size of the card.

A sleeve is even easier to make. It's just a fold of card, paper or other material, which can be fastened at the sides or top with pins, glue, laces, strings, mini pegs and so on. It's a great way to use all those cardmaking scraps which you can't bear to throw away

HAPPY BIRTHDAY TO YOU

Although it's tiny, this card is a feast of different textures simply layered together

Finished size

2³/₄ x 3¹/₂in (7 x 9cm)

You will need...

Materials

- Fold of white corrugated card, 2³/₄ x 3¹/₂in (7 x 9cm)
- Blue angel hair, 2 x 2¹/₄in (5 x 6cm)
- Scrap of translucent writing paper
- Gel pen, deep pink
- Pink paper flower
- Yellow bow
- Small yellow punched paper flower
- 12in (30cm) fine bead braid

Glue

- Double-sided adhesive tape
- PVA adhesive

Equipment

- Scissors

Crafty Touch

Ring the changes by using sheet music or printed text in place of the handwritten panel on this card.

1 Attach the blue angel hair panel to folded card with double-sided tape.

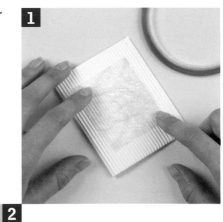

2 Write 'happy birthday' in deep pink gel pen on a scrap of writing paper. Tear the panel to 1¹/₂ x 2in (4 x 6cm) and attach to the blue panel with double-sided tape.

3 Glue the pink flower, bow and small punched yellow flower into position.

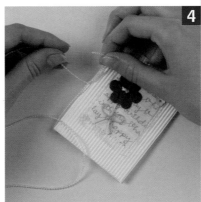

4 Tie decorative bead braid around the card and add a dab of adhesive to secure the knot.

FLOWER IN MY POCKET

Let your fashion fancy run free and make this cute jeans pocket, complete with flower and 'happy birthday' tag

Finished size
3³/₄ x 5in (9.5 X 13cm)

You will need...

Materials
- Fold of mauve card
  3³/₄ x 5in (9.5 x 13cm)
- Pink mesh 2¹/₂ x 4in
  (6.5 x 10.5cm)
- Scrap of thin denim
- Scrap of patterned ribbon
- Yellow flower shape
- 1in (3cm) length of green
  paper cord
- Light green gel pen
- Red jewel
- Small heart shape
- Three flower sequins
- Butterfly
- Tiny bow
- 'Happy birthday' tag

Glue
- Sticky foam pads
- Double-sided adhesive tape
- PVA adhesive

Equipment
- Small scissors

Crafty Touch

This versatile design is great
for using all those super
scraps of ribbon and tiny
sequins you've been saving
for a special project, so don't
hesitate to shower it with
trimmings!

1 Trace the pocket
template onto denim and
cut out. Attach a strip of
patterned ribbon at the top
with double-sided tape.

2 Add 'stitches' with light
green pen then glue the
flower sequins and heart into
place.

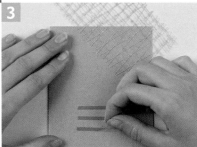

3 Invisibly attach the pink
mesh to the mauve card
by placing strips of double-
sided tape in the area where
the pocket will go. Attach the
pocket with sticky pads.

4 Glue a green stalk in the
pocket and attach the
flower head with small sticky
pads at each side of the stalk.

5 Glue a jewel in the centre
of the flower and add the
butterfly, small bow and
message tag.

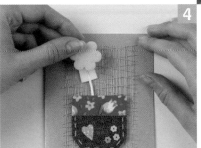

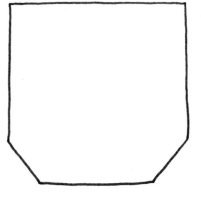

PRETTY PETALS

Flowers are a wonderful way of saying that you care, and this tactile design with its yellow silk rose, pearls and silky ribbon is sure to delight

Finished size
4¼ x 6in (10.5 x 15cm)

You will need...

Materials
- Fold of white card 4¼ x 6in (10.5 x 15cm)
- Fold of pink transparent paper, 4¼ x 6in (10.5 x 15cm)
- Length of green silky gingham ribbon, at least 8in (20cm)
- Three small pink paper hearts
- Green pearl braid, 3in (8cm)
- Deep pink Accent beads
- Small yellow silk rose

Glue
- Double-sided adhesive tape
- PVA adhesive
- Sticky foam pad

Equipment
- Small scissors
- Scallop scissors

Crafty Touch

Ribbon and silk flowers are available in so many styles and colours that you could make this design many times over and it would look different each and every time. For an extra helping of romance, why not trim it with coloured lace?

1 With scallop scissors, trim ½in (1.5cm) from the opening edge of the white folded card. Place the fold of pink paper inside and trim this too, in layers, then fix in place with double-sided tape.

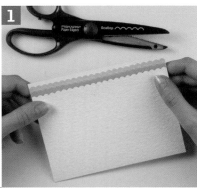

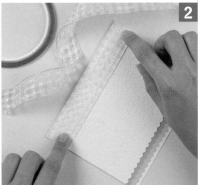

2 Place strips of double-sided tape next to the fold and press the ribbon into place. Trim off and keep the excess. Use a gel pen to enhance the ribbon design – here I've added pink dots.

3 Remove the plastic centre from the rose, add a dab of adhesive and sprinkle with pink Accent beads. Tap to remove excess. When the glue is dry attach the rose with a sticky pad.

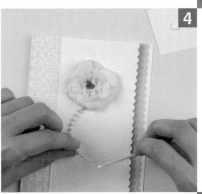

4 Tuck the pearl braid stem under the rose and secure with adhesive at the top and bottom.

5 Bond a scrap of ribbon to white card with double-sided tape. Cut two leaves and glue in place then add the three pink paper hearts.

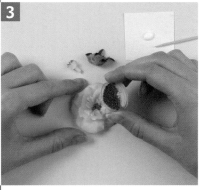

FLYING HIGH

Take a blue sky, a colourful kite and a duo of tiny birds
and you have all the ingredients for a happy card, be it for
a birthday or just to say 'hello!'

Finished size
3³/₄ x 5¹/₄in (9.5 x 13.5cm)

You will need...

Materials
- Fold of blue card,
  3³/₄ x 5¹/₄in (9.5 x 13.5cm)
- Sheet of yellow
  corrugated card
- Scrap paper
- Red craft wire, 7in (18cm)
- Three small flowers
- Two bird sequins
- Pink silky thread

Glue
- Double-sided adhesive tape
- Sticky foam pads
- PVA adhesive

Equipment
- Small scissors
- Scallop scissors
- Round-nose pliers

Crafty Touch

Why not make a multi-coloured or a patterned kite? This design is ideal for trying out exciting new colourways.

1 Cut scalloped strips of yellow corrugated card and attach to the blue folded card with double-sided tape.

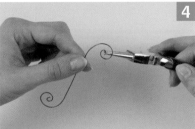

2 Cut four squares of corrugated card, 1³/₄in (4.5cm), and glue onto scrap paper, as shown.

3 Trace the template and draw the kite on corrugated card, ensuring that the cross of the cards is at the centre, then cut out.

4 Make a scroll from red wire and attach it to the back of the kite with double-sided tape.

5 Knot a few strands of pink silky thread together and tape them to the back of the kite.

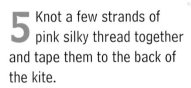

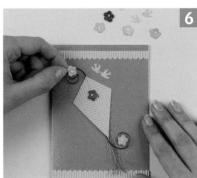

6 With sticky pads, fix the kite onto the card, then glue on flowers and bird sequins.

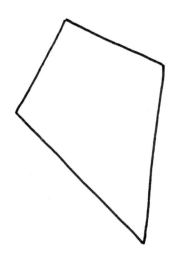

A LITTLE LOVE

Small, neat and sweet describes this design. It's perfect for birthdays, 'get well soon' or just to carry a message of love

Finished size

3 x 3½in (8 x 9cm)

You will need...

Materials

- Fold of ivory card,
  3 x 3½in (8 x 9cm)
- Deckle-edged panel of
  orange pearl card,
  2¼ x 2¾in (6 x 7cm)
- Two pieces of yellow angel
  hair, 1½ x 2in (4 x 5cm)
- Scrap of white corrugated
  card
- Three small flower heads
- Fine green paper yarn
- Tiny yellow bow
- Tiny 'with love' tag
- Sparkle gel pens, pink and
  yellow
- Pearl 3D paint

Glue

- Double-sided adhesive tape
- PVA adhesive

Equipment

- Small scissors
- Deckle scissors

Crafty Touch

Small ready-made flowers
can be bought as cake
decorations, so why not try
some out on this design?

1 Attach the orange panel
to the fold of ivory card
with double-sided tape then
add two layers of yellow
angel hair. Decorate the
edges of the orange panel
with pink gel pen dots.

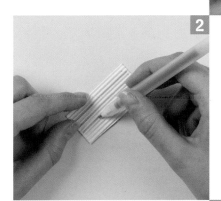

2 Add coloured stripes to a
scrap of corrugated card
and cut a vase shape,
½ x 1¼in (1.5 x 3cm).

3 For the flower stalks,
take three lengths of fine
green paper yarn, 1½in
(3.5cm), and thread into
corrugated flutes at the top of
the vase.

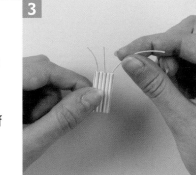

4 Attach the vase with
double-sided tape. Glue
the flower heads, message
tag and tiny bow in place then
add dots of 3D pearl paint to
the flower centres.

GROOVY BABY

Let's leave soft pinks and blues behind with this groovy and colourful design. It's the perfect welcome card for today's trendy babes!

44

Finished size
4 x 4½in (10 x 11.5 cm)

You will need...

Materials
- Fold of yellow corrugated card, 4 x 4½in (10 x 11.5 cm)
- Mauve pearl card panel with wavy, hand-cut edges 2½ x 2¾in (6.5 x 7cm)
- Four small punched flower shapes in assorted colours
- Two larger punched flower shapes in yellow
- Small heart shape
- White corrugated card
- Selection of felt brush pens and gel pens
- Green pearl braid
- Small piece of pink craft wire

Glue
- Double-sided adhesive tape
- PVA adhesive

Equipment
- Small scissors
- Scallop scissors
- Large and small flower punches (a corner punch is ideal as it makes two flower sizes)
- Round-nose pliers

Crafty Touch

By using different colours you can completely change a design. Try using just white and silver for the perfect Christening card.

1 Trim the opening edge of the folded card with scallop scissors. Attach a mauve trim using double-sided tape.

2 Attach the mauve panel with double-sided tape. Glue a small flower at each corner and add 'stitches' in light green gel pen.

3 Colour scraps of white corrugated card. Cut out two shapes to make the body and the hood of the pram.

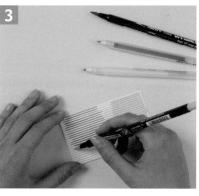

4 Make wire curl for pram handle and attach with tape on reverse of pram body. Glue pram body to mauve panel then add pram hood.

5 Glue pearl braid, heart and wheels in place, and add a pen dot in the centre of each wheel.

HAPPY DOG

This cheery chappie keeps finding his way into my designs, so I've dressed him up and sent him off with a letter to deliver!

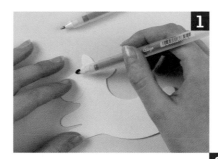

Finished size
4¼ x 5¼in (10.5 x 13.5cm)

You will need...

Materials
- Fold of red card, 4¼ x 5¼in (10.5 x 13.5cm)
- White card or watercolour paper, 3½ x 4¾in (9 x 12cm)
- Red gingham ribbon
- Scraps of yellow, red and pink pearl paper
- Small yellow pom-pom
- Black glaze gel pen
- Pink sparkle gel pen

Glue
- Double-sided adhesive tape
- PVA adhesive
- Sticky foam pads

Equipment
- Small scissors
- Small flower punch

Crafty Touch

Experiment with your own ideas for dressing this friendly canine character. Perhaps you'd like him to deliver a bunch of flowers instead of a letter!

1 Trace the dog template onto white card or watercolour paper and cut out. Add eyes and a nose in black pen and trim ears and toes in pink.

2 Bond gingham ribbon onto a scrap of paper with double-sided tape. Trace the coat and hat templates on the reverse, cut them out and attach with double-sided tape.

3 Trace the envelope template and cut from pink paper. Fold the envelope into shape then trim with a tiny red heart and place it in the dog's mouth.

4 Cut out the heart and flower trimmings and glue them onto the coat. Glue the yellow pom-pom onto the hat.

5 Use sticky pads to attach your Happy Dog to the folded red card.

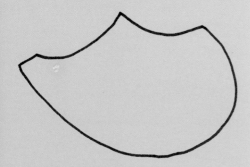

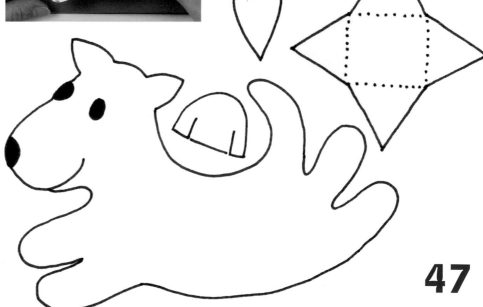

47

HOME SWEET HOME

Lighten someone's moving-day angst with this
cute design. It's sure to raise a smile!

Finished size

3³/₄ x 4¹/₃in (9.5 x 11cm)

You will need...

Materials

- Fold of lime green embossed card, 3³/₄ x 4¹/₃in (9.5 x 11cm)
- Scrap of red perforated card
- Scraps of white finely corrugated card
- Scraps of white, pink and mauve paper or card
- Pink craft wire, 4³/₄in (12cm)
- Yellow felt brush pen

Glue

- Double-sided adhesive tape
- PVA adhesive
- Sticky foam pads

Equipment

- Small scissors
- Round-nose pliers

1 Bond red perforated card to white paper. Trace the roof template and cut out.

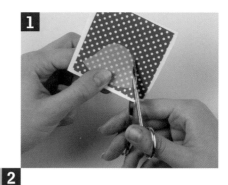

2 Lightly colour white corrugated card with yellow felt pen. Trace the toadstool base and chimney templates and cut them out.

3 Glue the toadstool together then add the door and heart.

4 Make pink wire curls and attach these to the rear of the chimney with double-sided tape.

5 Use sticky pads to attach the toadstool to the card and add a tiny 'sold' sign.

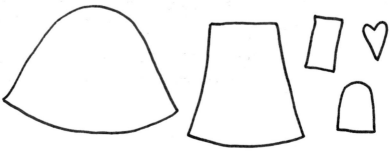

Crafty Touch

If you haven't got any red perforated paper for the toadstool you could use a white gel pen or pearl 3D paint to make spots on red paper.

COSY CAT

Friends who are feline fanatics will adore this
portrait of a cosily curled up cat

Finished size
4³/₄in (12cm) square

You will need...

Materials
- Fold of pink textured card, 4³/₄in (12cm) square
- Deckle-edged frame in mauve, 3in (8cm) square
- Green embossed card panel, 2³/₄in (7cm) square
- Green paper cord or string, 3in (8cm)
- Stick-on flower jewel, mauve
- Tiny paper flower
- Scrap of white watercolour paper
- Felt brush pens or coloured pencils, tan, blue and pink
- White, yellow and pink gel pens
- Pink sparkle gel pen

Glue
- Double-sided adhesive tape
- PVA adhesive
- Sticky foam pads

Equipment
- Small scissors
- Stylus or empty ball-point pen

Crafty Touch

If this is a special card for a proud moggie owner, do take care to colour the cat accordingly!

1 Trace the templates and, using the stylus, draw the cat's head and body on watercolour paper. Colour lightly with pens or crayons then cut them out and glue together.

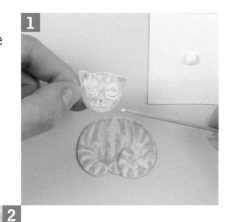

2 Decorate a mauve frame with gel pen dots then attach the green card panel and green cord loop on the reverse using double-sided tape.

3 Fix the frame in the centre of the pink card using sticky pads then add the stick-on flower jewel.

4 Attach the cat with a sticky pad and tuck the flower into its tail, adding a dot of adhesive to secure.

SWEET AND SIMPLE

I love creams and browns, but I also love glitz, so I've added an orange
trim and wire curls to bring subtle glamour to these simple shapes

Finished size
4 x 4³/₄in (10 x 12cm)

You will need...

Materials
- Fold of cream textured card, 4 x 4³/₄in (10 x 12cm)
- Orange pearl card, ³/₄ x 5in (2 x 13cm)
- Two corrugated flower die-cuts, one cream, one light brown
- Scrap of gold paper
- Orange paper covered wire, 3¹/₂in (9cm)
- Orange craft wire, 4in (10cm)
- Bronze gel-pen

Glue
- Double-sided adhesive tape
- PVA adhesive
- Sticky foam pads

Equipment
- Scissors
- Wavy scissors
- Round-nose pliers

Crafty Touch

If you like the natural look, this design could be created with dried flowers and handmade papers.

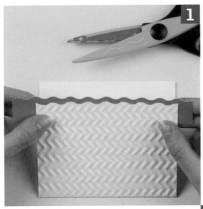

1 With wavy scissors, cut a ¹/₃in (1cm) strip from the opening edge of the folded card. Add orange trim using double-sided adhesive tape, and decorate the edge with a bronze pen.

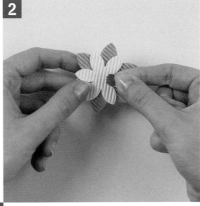

2 Glue the cream flower onto the light brown flower, then add torn gold paper in the centre.

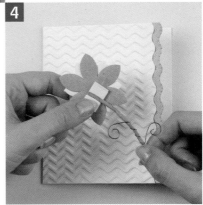

3 Wind the wire around the paper covered wire stem, finishing with a curl at each side.

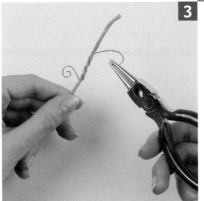

4 Attach the stem to the reverse of the flower with double-sided tape, then place a sticky pad either side of the stem and fix the flower onto the card.

PALE AND INTERESTING

Pick out a perfect accent colour and then pale
will indeed be interesting!

Finished size

3¹/₂ x 4³/₄in (9 x 12cm)

You will need...

Materials

- Fold of white textured card, 3¹/₂ x 4³/₄in (9 x 12cm)
- Three small pale blue fabric flowers
- Scrap of blue textured pearl paper
- Pale blue craft wire, 4in (10cm)
- Turquoise madeira thread

Glue

- PVA adhesive
- Double-sided adhesive tape

Equipment

- Small scissors
- Darning needle and mousemat
- Round-nose pliers

Crafty Touch

Add a couple of wedding bells for a delightful wedding card.

1 With a darning needle, and resting on the reverse of a mousemat, make a hole at the top left corner of the card. Pass a loop of turquoise threads through the hole then knot, adding a dab of adhesive to secure.

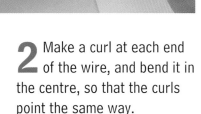

2 Make a curl at each end of the wire, and bend it in the centre, so that the curls point the same way.

3 Fix the wire curl onto card with double-sided tape, then attach the flowers.

4 Cut leaves from pearl textured paper, add a dab of adhesive to the base of each one and tuck under the flowers.

SNOWY CHRISTMAS

**For special seasonal greetings take inspiration
from your dreams of a snowy white Christmas**

60

Finished size
3¹/₃ x 5¹/₂in (8.5 x 14cm)

You will need...

Materials
- Fold of white textured card, 3¹/₃ x 5¹/₂in (8.5 x 14cm)
- Scrap of white perforated card
- Scrap of white and gold sparkly paper
- Three green skeleton leaves
- Scrap of gold paper
- Scrap of smooth white card
- Fine green pen
- Ultra-fine black pen

Glue
- Double-sided adhesive tape
- PVA adhesive

Equipment
- Small scissors

Crafty Touch

Using the templates this snowy landscape can be made from any sheet craft material, from foam to fabric.

1 Trace the hill templates and cut out from perforated card and sparkly paper. Glue these in position, aligning with the folded edge, then trim opening edge if necessary.

2 Trace the tree templates and cut from skeleton leaves, then lightly glue into place.

3 Write your greeting on a scrap of white card. Cut this out and decorate the edges with green pen.

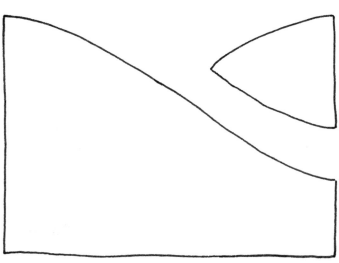

4 Attach the greeting to gold paper using double-sided tape, then cut out again and fix at the corner of the card.

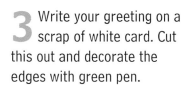

STAMP OF LOVE

Use pretty mini stamps on little wooden tiles
to convey your message of love

62

Finished size
4 x 5in (10 x 13cm)

You will need...

Materials
- Fold of cream card, 4 x 5in (10 x 13cm)
- Jute ribbon, 4³/₄in (12cm)
- Scrap of lightweight wood veneer
- White crayon
- Orange ink pad
- Gold sparkle gel pen

Glue
- Double-sided adhesive tape

Equipment
- Small 'with love' rubber stamp
- Small potted tulip rubber stamp
- Scissors

Crafty Touch

I've cut the wooden tiles from a piece of lightweight wood veneer but you can try rubber stamping onto lots of different materials, from foam to fabric. You'll be amazed at the results.

1 Stamp the message and flower motifs onto a scrap of wood veneer and cut out to form small tiles.

2 Add sketchy white areas around stamped images using a white crayon, then add gold dots to each corner.

3 Attach jute ribbon to the folded card with strips of double-sided tape, then attach the wooden tiles.

CHEERY CHICKEN

Lilac and yellow? A fine fat hen on a nest? It must be Easter!

Finished size
4 x 5³/₄in (10 x 14.5cm)

You will need...

Materials
- Fold of lilac textured card, 4 x 5³/₄in (10 x 14.5cm)
- Pale blue card, 2 x 2in (5 x 5cm)
- Scraps of white corrugated card
- Scrap of orange pearl paper
- Four small mauve flowers
- Yellow flat paper yarn
- Yellow felt brush pen
- Brown felt brush pen
- Blue seed bead

Glue
- Double-sided adhesive tape
- PVA adhesive
- Sticky foam pads

Equipment
- Scissors

Crafty Touch

Change the card panels for gingham and jute ribbon, and you have the perfect country-style birthday card.

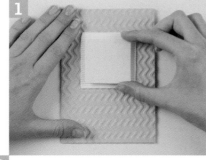

1 Colour grooves of white corrugated card with yellow felt pen. Cut panel, 2¹/₄in (6cm) square, and attach to folded lilac card with double-sided tape. Attach light blue panel with sticky pads.

2 Glue a mauve flower at each corner of the light blue panel.

3 Colour grooves of white corrugated card with brown felt pen. Trace the hen template and cut out.

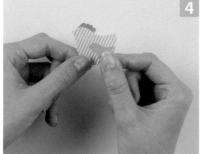

4 Using templates, cut trimmings for the hen from orange paper and glue in place, then add a blue seed bead for the eye.

5 Attach the hen to the light blue panel with a sticky pad and glue small pieces of yellow paper yarn around it to form the nest.

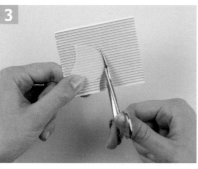

SEALED WITH A KISS

A silver heart and just one embroidered kiss is the perfect way to
send a sophisticated message of love to that special person

Finished size

3¹/₂ x 5¹/₂in (9 x 14cm)

You will need...

Materials

- Fold of white silk card, 3¹/₂ x 5¹/₂in (9 x 14cm)
- Torn panel of brown paper, 1³/₄ x 2in (4.5 x 5cm)
- Length of coiled silver effect wire
- Scrap of white card
- A few small iridescent cellophane flowers
- Silver madeira thread

Glue

- Double-sided adhesive tape
- PVA adhesive

Equipment

- Scissors
- Paper crimper
- Sewing needle

Crafty Touch

This fascinating coiled craft effect wire is available in a wide range of colours so why not try styling it in red for your Valentine!

1 Feed the panel of brown paper through the crimper to make a grooved effect and attach to folded card with double-sided tape.

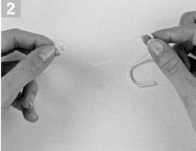

2 Make a heart from silver effect wire by stretching the wire slightly then forming a small ball.

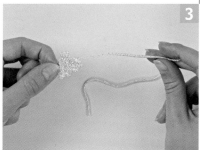

3 Flatten the wire ball and keep loosely winding the wire around it. Start to form a heart, keeping it fairly flat.

4 When your heart shape is complete, use double-sided tape to attach it to the brown panel.

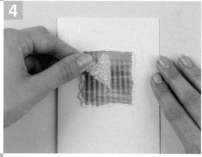

5 Make a cross stitch in silver thread on white card, then tear it out and glue in place.

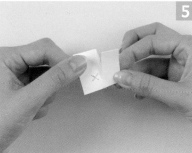

6 Glue cellophane flowers onto the panel.

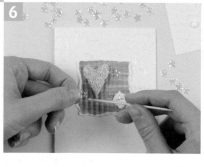

IN THE PINK

This is really a sunflower motif but I'm so happy when I'm cardmaking that I view the world through rose-tinted spectacles and I decided to colour it pink!

Finished size
4 x 5³/₄in (10 x 14.5cm)

You will need...

Materials
- Fold of white card,
  4 x 5³/₄in (10 x 14.5cm)
- Scrap of white watercolour
  paper
- Torn panel of pink
  translucent paper,
  2³/₄ x 3¹/₃in (7 x 8.5cm)
- Silver madeira thread
- Fine pink pen
- Ultra-fine black pen
- Pink, orange and green
  stamp pads
- Mini sponge applicators
- Silver heart paper-fastener

Glue
- Double-sided adhesive tape
- Sticky foam pads

Equipment
- Scissors
- Paper crimper
- Brass stencil, sunflower
  design
- Light box
- Ball-end embossing stylus

Crafty Touch

If you prefer to use peel-off
lettering or a rubber stamp
for your greeting, just add it
at the top of the card.

1 Feed pink translucent
paper through the
crimper for a grooved effect,
then attach to the folded card
with double-sided tape that is
placed where it will be
concealed by motifs.

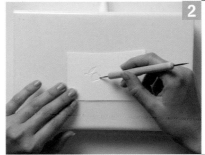

2 Emboss the sunflower
motif onto a scrap of
white watercolour paper,
using the light box, stylus and
brass stencil.

3 Keeping the stencil in
place, gently add colour
with mini sponge applicators
and ink pads, blending the
pink and orange.

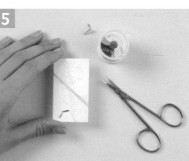

4 Cut a panel around the
sunflower, 1¹/₄ x 2¹/₂in
(3.5 x 6.5cm) and decorate
the edges with fine pink pen.

5 Add strands of silver
thread at corners of
panel, press silver heart into
place, then fix onto pink panel
with sticky pads.

6 On scraps of watercolour
paper, write a tiny
birthday message and kisses,
then attach to the finished
card with small pieces of
sticky pad.

SUPER SMOOTH

The smooth, cushioned look of this die-cut silver flower
reminds me of a piece of jewellery and it is just right for customising
with a tangle of hot pink wire and cool turquoise beads

Finished size
4 x 5½in (10 x 14cm)

You will need...

Materials

- Fold of turquoise card, 4 x 5½in (10 x 14cm)
- Scrap of white card
- Scrap of bright pink handmade paper
- Corrugated silver die-cut flower
- Four blue flower sequins
- Pink effect wire
- A few turquoise seed beads

Glue

- Double-sided adhesive tape
- PVA adhesive
- Sticky foam pad

Equipment

- Scissors

Crafty Touch

Try cutting a flower for this design from different materials such as sparkly foam or holographic card.

1 Tear a panel of white card, 1¾in (4.5cm) square, and a panel of pink handmade paper, slightly smaller, then layer onto folded turquoise card with double-sided tape.

2 Glue a flower sequin at each corner of the panel.

3 Take a silver die-cut flower, smooth side upwards, and wind pink effect wire loosely between the petals and across the centre, adding a few beads as you progress. Secure the end of the wire on the reverse of the flower with tape.

4 Use a sticky pad to attach the flower to the centre panel.

SUNNY DAYS

Everyone should have sunshine, blue skies and flowers on their birthday!

Finished size
4 x 5in (10 x 13cm)

You will need...

Materials
- Fold of white card, 4 x 5in (10 x 13cm)
- Panel of pink glitter card with wavy edges, 2³/₄ x 4in (7 x 10cm)
- Scrap of watercolour paper
- Scrap of white glitter card
- Scrap of orange glitter card
- Green paper cord
- Pink paper cord
- Turquoise felt brush pen
- Three red plastic self-adhesive flowers
- 'Happy birthday' motif
- 4³/₄in (12cm) of gold craft wire

Glue
- Double-sided adhesive tape
- Sticky foam pads

Equipment
- Scissors
- Scallop scissors
- Darning needle and mousemat
- Round-nose pliers

Crafty Touch

If time is short there are lots of tiny ready-made flowers and sun motifs available which would suit this versatile design.

1 Use turquoise felt pen to colour watercolour paper then cut out a panel, about 2³/₄in x 2in (7 x 5cm), with wavy sides and a scallop effect at the top and bottom.

2 Rest on a mousemat to make six holes in the panel with a darning needle. Pass pink paper cord through the holes to make stitches.

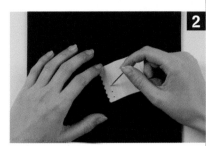

3 For stems, thread three pieces of green paper cord, 1¹/₄in (3.5cm), through the pink stitches.

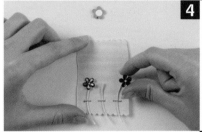

4 Using adhesive patches on the reverse of the flowers to attach them to the stems.

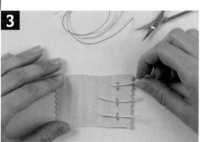

5 Make a sun motif from orange and white glitter card, and make a 'happy birthday' panel. Attach these with double-sided tape.

6 Make a scroll in gold craft wire and attach it to the back of the sun with double-sided tape.

7 Use sticky pads to fix the turquoise panel onto the pink glitter panel. Fix these onto folded white card with sticky pads.

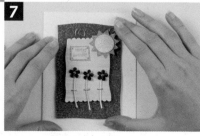

The card reads: with love on your special day

A MESSAGE OF LOVE

Delight someone on their special day with this colourful message of love

Finished size

4 x 5¼in (10 x 13.5cm)

You will need...

Materials

- Fold of green pearl card, 4 x 5¼in (10 x 13.5cm)
- Scraps of orange card
- Pink batik die-cut flower with centre
- Yellow paper-covered wire
- Flat yellow paper yarn
- Ultra-fine transparent yellow glitter

Glue

- Narrow double-sided adhesive tape
- Regular double-sided adhesive tape
- PVA adhesive

Equipment

- Scissors

Crafty Touch

These batik die-cut flowers are so easy to customize that you'll get a fabulous result every time.

1 Lay strips of narrow double-sided tape across the top and bottom of the green folded card. Peel away the protective layer and pour glitter over the adhesive.

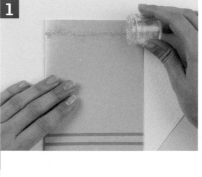

2 Lay strips of double-sided tape across the back of the flower to hold the central die-cut in place then attach it to the front of the card.

3 Make a spiral of yellow paper-covered wire and secure in the centre of the flower with glue.

4 Cover a scrap of orange card with double-sided adhesive tape and sprinkle it with glitter. Cut six leaves and a few circles in various sizes.

5 Add a dab of glue to the base of each leaf and tuck behind the flower, then add a few circles.

6 Take four strands of flat yellow paper yarn and tie around the fold, then glue the knot to secure it.

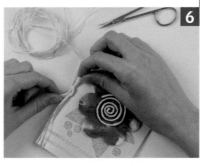

HEART'S DELIGHT

Whether you are congratulating a happy couple on their wedding day or making a whole batch of invitations, this simple design will fit the bill

Finished size
4 x 5in (10 x 13cm)

You will need...

Materials
- Fold of thick, smooth watercolour paper, 4 x 5in (10 x 13cm)
- Scraps of same
- Gold Japan thread, $6^{1}/_{3}$ft (2m)
- A few gold and glass beads
- Brass stencil with heart design

Glue
- Double-sided adhesive tape
- PVA adhesive
- Sticky foam pad

Equipment
- Scissors
- Light box
- Ball-end embossing stylus

Crafty Touch

Use silver thread and crystal beads for a silver wedding anniversary card.

1 Emboss the heart motif onto a scrap of white watercolour paper, using the light box, stylus, and brass stencil. Cut out the heart.

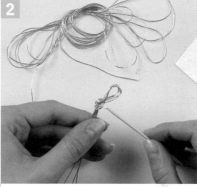

2 Bunch four 12in (30cm) strands of gold Japan thread, double and tie them in a knot, forming a small loop and tassel effect. Add a dab of glue to the reverse of the knot.

3 Fix the tassel onto the back of the heart with double-sided tape and trim the ends of the thread.

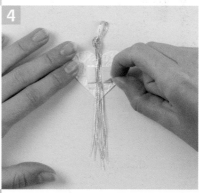

4 Place a sticky pad either side of the gold threads and fix the heart onto folded card, then add a dab of adhesive to the back of the knot to secure it.

5 Thread the gold beads onto the gold thread, knotting loosely between each bead. Tie onto the folded card and secure with a dab of adhesive.

USEFUL ADDRESSES

Artoz
Decorative paper, perforated card and translucent paper:
www.londongraphics.co.uk

Craft King
Discounted crafts of all kinds.
Tel: 1 800 769 9494, or go to:
www.craftking.com

Hobbycraft
A wide range of high quality craft materials including glitter, wire, wooden doves and Madeira threads: www.hobbycraft.co.uk

Impex
Hi-tack double-sided adhesive tapes, Accent and seed beads. Visit:
www.impexcreativecrafts.co.uk

Lakeland
Plastic jewel flowers, textured card, rubber stamps, decorative braids, die-cut card. For mail order details go to: www.lakelandlimited.com

LJ Gibbs
Paper and card, paper-covered wire, paper string, effect wire, die-cut flowers, decorative meshes and ribbons. For mail order details phone: 44 (0)1959 533663, or go to: www.ljgibbsandpartners.com

Markingworld
For Sakura Gelly Roll pens, contact Markingworld on:
44 (0)1360 661098 for nearest stockist, or go to:
www.markingworld.com

Paperdeluxe
Hand-dyed paper cords, paper yarns and die-cut dolphin motifs.
Details available from:
paperdeluxe@hotmail.com

Personal Impressions
Stamp pads, foam applicators, scissors, brass stencils, Marvy Le Plume II brush pens, glitter, craft wire and round-nose pliers.
Tel: 44 (0)1787 375241,
or go to: www.richstamp.co.uk

Sunshine Discount Crafts
Stocks a wide range of discounted craft items, including card and envelope sets.
Tel: 1 800 729 2878, or visit:
www.sunshinecrafts.com

INDEX